D1759524

100
HEARTWARMING SHORT STORIES
FOR SENIORS

Easy-to-read, Cheerful, and Loving Stories

to celebrate Life's Treasures

Published By:

Feel Good Publishing

Table of Contents

Foreword

This collection of short stories has been crafted to bring warmth to your soul like a cup of tea on a chilly morning. Some of the stories may feel like a trip down memory lane, helping with cognitive stimulation by reminding you of some of your own cherished moments from your life.

Enjoy the benefits of an improved memory by retelling the simple plots of these stories to friends and family, or start a book club where you can discuss the stories and formulate your own exciting adventurous endings—like some of the characters in this book. Find creative ways to make your reading journey more exciting for you.

The book is divided into themes so that you can choose what you feel like reading whenever you pick it up. Other stories are simply there to give you a good laugh—or at least a soft chuckle or smile—while others explore ideas and themes of love, loss, and different emotions we go through in life.

My sincere hope is that as you go through these pages, your mind will be refreshed and renewed each time, harnessing positive feelings and thoughts. I hope you put this book down feeling good about being at the top of the wisdom ladder as a senior, a grandparent perhaps, a parent, or simply a member of the community.

You have worked hard throughout your life. Now, it's time to sit back, relax, and enjoy a simple, easy-to-read, and exciting journey through these stories.

Enjoy

Your Free Gift

Hey there! Thank you so much for choosing my book and I hope you enjoy reading the stories. In appreciation of your support, I have created 3 FREE Bonuses. You can get instant access by signing up for my email newsletter. In addition to the FREE Bonus content, you will be added to my

Exclusive Elite Reader Program!

You are entitled to ALL of the below:

- Exclusive access to all my forthcoming book publications
- FREE Book Giveaway
- FREE bonus content
- AND…. So Much More!!

All the bonus content is 100% free. You do not need to provide any personal information apart from your email address:

To get access to all content FOR FREE

Just Click Here

Or Scan the QR Code

Bonus #1 Serene Landscapes Coloring Book

Inside the book, you will discover:

- Curated coloring pages, all hand drawn by our creative team.
- Large print design, suitable for either beginners or seasoned artists
- Helps to increase focus, a relaxing way to step away from the digital world!

If you are interested in this book, then make sure to grab a free copy!

Bonus #2 Mindful Meditation for Everyday Living

Inside the book, you will discover:

- Benefits associated with meditation.
- How to start meditation as a complete beginner.
- Aging gracefully with daily mediation practice
- And Much More!!

If you are interested in this book, then make sure to grab a free copy!

Bonus #3 We Love Gardening

Inside the book, you will discover:

- A comprehensive guide to all about evergreen gardening.
- Benefits of Gardening for kids.
- How to arrange your backyard landscaping.
- Flower Gardening
- And Much More!!

If you are interested in this book, then make sure to grab a free copy!

Chapter 1

Life's Hidden Gems

DISCOVER THE BEAUTIFUL TREASURE INSIDE

Mosaic Memories

Encouraged by the warm breeze of spring, Julie decided that it was the perfect time to clear out her closet, and she called on Emma, her granddaughter, to help. A box wrapped in mosaic paper was sticking out and caught her eye. She motioned to Emma to pull it out.

Emma flung it out as though expecting it to be heavy, and the box soared through the air with its contents spilling all over the carpet and bed.

"Grandma! Is that you?" Emma cried.

She rushed over to pick up one of the photographs that had fallen out of the box, a huge smile spreading across her face.

Chuckling, Julie responded, "My dear, I always told you I was a stunner back in my day!"

She suddenly had a faraway look on her face, thinking of the days when she would go dancing with her girls and one day meet her beloved underneath the moonlight on a night out. *What a perfect gentleman he was*, she thought quietly to herself.

Her granddaughter walked over to her and gave her a warm hug, which both comforted Julie but also gave her a deep sense of gratitude for the beautiful life she has lived.

The Robots

Warm-spirited feelings rushed through Fiona's body. It made her feel as if she was dancing, as loud laughter spilled from her lungs. The image of her two older sisters, Mary and Kathrine, dancing to jazz music flashed in her mind. *They were so robotic,* she remembered, smiling.

Her son came into the room at this moment and inquisitively looked over his mother's shoulder to see what was amusing her. "Goodness! They look like robots," he gasped. "Were they good dancers or was this just a pose for the camera?"

Fiona smiled and nodded, "Oh, yes, but they were awfully troublesome also."

"Really?"

"Terribly so! They'd practice dancing in our room every evening, and when our mother banned them from doing it because of the racket it would cause, they'd sneak out the window!"

He grinned cheekily, "And you would help them, wouldn't you?"

"Well, yes. They always spoiled me with some sweet treats after, but all I really wanted was to go dancing with them."

Her son held out his hand, nodding his head to encourage his mother to take up his invitation. Fiona reached out to him, slowly getting up from her seat. And for some moments, they laughed and danced the night away.

The Last Adventure

For much of his life, Norman had craved something no one else could quite understand. He had an unshakeable, deep desire to fly—something he was undoubtedly mercilessly teased for growing up. Well, today was the day he would finally get as close as he could to his life-long dream.

Having arrived at his destination a good hour and a half too early, he checked his wristwatch for what must have been the seventh time and let out a silent shriek of excitement because it was finally time!

He walked as briskly as he could to the counter, and the lovely little lady at the reception had a concerned look on her face and asked, "Sir, how may I help you? I believe you may be lost?"

Norman eagerly shook his head, "No, my dear. I'm Norman, we spoke on the phone and I scheduled an appointment for 2:15–"

"Norman!" the woman exclaimed. "Yes, of course! You're skydiving today. I must say, I don't often see your peers in these parts," she chimed, smiling gleefully.

"Well, my dear, I hope this shows you it's never too late to go after your dreams. I have always wanted to fly and this is as close as I will get!

The Lemonade

Bob pushed his empty glass of lemonade aside, stretched his leg out under the table, and asked Halle if she remembered the time they almost moved to Hawaii. Halle's face lit up with a smile as he watched her tuck a stray strand behind her ear.

"Well if we had moved, it would have been terrible, really," she said, matter-of-factly.

Bob grinned, "How so?"

"For starters, we were readying to move that summer break, right?"

Bob nodded, though he seemed to remember that the move was during the winter break.

"Well, Tyler lost Mr. X around that time," Halle continued.

"...Mr. X?"

Halle nodded, sipping her lemonade. "Mr. X—that old stuffed animal who wore an orange vest and green bandana?"

Bob nodded with a smile on his face, as he was certain the stuffed animal was a pirate figurine.

"Well, imagine what Tyler would've been like while traveling! And don't get me started on Krissy. You remember, don't you?"

"Yes, we said that she could attend camp for the first time," he agreed. "In the end, we were always meant to be here."

"Oh, if we had moved, Julie would've never met Mark," Halle said as she watched her grandson wobble as he ran between his mom and dad.

Down the Garden Path

At this time of day, the garden was enveloped in a misty glow as the sun began to set. Throughout the years, it had become much like a tradition for Daisy and her daughter to tend to the garden at this time, with a cool breeze filling the air instead of the treacherous heat.

Today's activity was partly a leisurely stroll down memory lane as they remembered all the memories they had made here. Hooking her hand through her daughter's arm, Daisy sighed and closed her eyes to soak in the sweet scents that filled the air. Glancing up at Petal, she beamed with excitement, anticipating the arrival of her first grandchild.

With two botanists for parents, the family tradition in Daisy's household was to name every child after a flower or a botanic theme. Petal had happily indulged in this tradition, which is what led them down the garden path on this day, looking for some inspiration.

Daisy giggled happily under her breath. It did not seem like long ago when Petal was running around the garden, jumping in puddles. *In a few short moments,* she thought, *I will have another little rascal jumping around in the puddles, too!*

Dancing Queens

Moira followed Erica into the bright classroom. They were immediately drawn to the group of children huddled in the corner by the large mirror. Moira elbowed Erica.

"...yes, yes, I notice them."

"They should mind themselves; we're not that old!" Moira said.

Erica burst into giggles, which sounded like a deflating balloon. The children found this hilarious and began to chuckle alongside her.

A young girl with short wispy curls ran over, cleared her throat, and straightened up into a ballerina's posture. "Hello, I'm Kim, are you our instructors for the day?"

Erica smiled. "I suppose you could call us inspectors."

"Inspectors?" both Moira and Kim exclaimed.

"Well, ballet has changed so much over time since we last danced, we're here to take the class alongside you and make sure it's up to par..." Erica explained.

"Alright everyone, places," the instructor announced.

Erica shrugged. "Here we go! We've always had beginner's luck anyway, remember that pottery class?"

Moira smiled. "You mean the way your vase spluttered all over the instructor's face? He struggled to get it out of his hair, you know."

The ladies laughed as they shuffled to stand in line in response to the instructor's signal, in preparation for yet another afternoon of fun.

Little Flutters in the Wind

While enjoying a relaxing morning on her porch and looking at the colorful daisies in her garden, Emma gasped as she saw two butterflies fluttering into her field of view. It was a beautiful sight to see, as they twirled around each other like a pair of lovers doing the waltz.

She smiled, remembering how excited her third graders would be whenever they saw butterflies in the playground—and the shock on their faces as she explained metamorphosis to them.

She began wondering just how quickly sweet moments like this in nature—and also in life—pass by quickly. Looking around at the trees and flowers, she thought of how they too would soon lose their luster under thick layers of snow. Yet, in her heart, she felt a deep sense of peace and gratitude for the experience, however fleeting, as well as many other memorable moments throughout her life that brought her immense joy.

Indeed, she thought, *a thing of beauty is not a joy forever. But it certainly gives moments of joy that can leave a lasting impression.*

The Sparrow's Song

After a long day filled with chatter and excitement, Greg decided to take a stroll through the park to relax. Some friends had dropped by for lunch and ended up staying over the whole afternoon as they enjoyed a game of cards together, passing time with stories from their youth.

He was compelled to stop along his path when he heard melodies coming from a branch not far from where he was. He looked up and saw a sparrow, standing tall and singing with his chest puffed, as though performing for a crowd. Greg decided to be the bird's audience and took a seat on a nearby park bench.

He began to think about how such a small creature survives in the unforgiving wilderness and comes out on the other side with a song that lifts his spirits. He remembered reading a story as a child about how sparrows are a symbol of resilience, freedom, and happiness in different cultures.

This short encounter reminded Greg of how nature is full of small wonders that give hope. He promised himself that he would come back to this bench as often as he could to simply sit, listen to, and appreciate the freely given magic of nature.

Seasons and Change

As her day progressed, Mary looked outside and longed for some fresh air after spending the whole morning catching up on some reading. The illustrious stories she enjoyed always inspired her to bring some of the scenes to life.

With her painting supplies and easel in hand, she decided to head to the forest. *How fortunate it is that I took the leap of faith and followed my dreams*, she thought as she recalled the time she quit her job at a law firm to do what brought her true joy.

She found the perfect spot: A clearing amid the maple trees. As she started working on her painting, she thought of how much the forest transformed throughout the year, with the ebbing and flowing of seasons, each one bringing its own charm and colors along with it.

She thought how very similar this was to her own life seasons. From childhood to becoming a teenager, an adult, and now aging gracefully. She appreciated that each season in her life brought something new and had its own charm.

Mary stopped for a moment and closed her eyes with her hands clasped to her chest. Then she breathed a sigh of gratitude and continued painting.

Life's Boundless Possibilities

For as long as she could remember, Sarah woke up at the crack of dawn so that she could start her day in front of a tranquil sunrise at the beach.

Today was no different. Her alarm went off at 5.00 a.m., but she was already awake and was preparing a cup of coffee to take with her on her morning promenade.

As she was walking toward the beach, the salty scent of the sea filled the air and she could hear the waves crashing as if to welcome her to her favorite place.

Sarah spent most of her life at sea. Her father was a sailor, and from a young age, he trained her in this work. She remembered her first encounter with the sea on a boat and the overwhelming feeling its vastness had given her. From that age, she had used this as a metaphor for the endless possibilities that awaited her on her journey of life if she was courageous enough to navigate the seas of her own life.

She was glad to realize that she had, in fact, done this. She had no regrets and only contentment filled her heart as she sipped her coffee and enjoyed the view.

Simple Pleasures and Daily Delights

Misty was always an adventurer from a young age—always seeking a thrill and the next best thing that would give her an adrenaline rush. Naturally, she traveled far and wide throughout her life, seeing incredible sights and doing the most daring things.

However, one thing she discovered through the years of excitement was that the quiet moments of stillness, and the simple things that made her smile, gave her a warm feeling that no thrill ever could. As time went on, she had moments of coming home to herself and learning to enjoy the quiet simple things in life.

As she sat on her porch sipping some chai tea, she laughed at the thought that once upon a time, she would not have found anything enticing about this. As the spicy tea aroma filled the air, she happily indulged all her senses, feeling the warmth from the tea, but also from her heart.

She now made it a point to share with anyone who would listen what she has learned: The simple things that are often taken for granted can be a bottomless reservoir of happiness if one only takes a moment to be fully present and enjoy them for what they are.

A Love Written in the Stars

Henry and Joanne believed that their love story was one of love at first sight. Ever since they met, they had been joined at the hip and did everything together. They had similar hobbies, and they enjoyed exploring the same things.

One such hobby was stargazing. They had invested in fancy telescopes and machines that would capture magnificent images of stars and nebulas. Their home library was filled with books on space exploration, and they continued to add to their collection if they came across something new.

When they built their home, they made sure to have a rooftop that would allow them to gaze at the sky on clear nights. As they were laying under the night sky one evening, Henry said, "My love, you know why I have always been fascinated by the universe? It reminds me of the vastness of life and the uncharted planes that exist. It's humbling to know that there is so much we do not know."

"But it's also exciting!" Joanne chimed in, as she turned to look at her husband with a smile on her face.

"Oh yes, absolutely," Henry replied. He took his wife's hand into his and they continued gazing well into the night.

The Firefly Promise

Jacob was sitting in his rocking chair one evening, reading the newspaper. His children had come to visit, and their daughter had insisted on staying the night with her grandparents. However, she was now pestering Jacob with never-ending questions and curiosities.

He was mildly irritated as he was looking forward to some quiet time in the evening to catch up on the news and smoke a cigar. But when he looked up from his newspaper, he saw tiny lights twinkling in the garden. When his granddaughter noticed his fixation, she looked over her shoulder and began gushing excitedly at the sight. She had never seen fireflies, and she was ecstatic. To her, they were like little fairies painting the flowers. Even Jacob was mesmerized by their graceful movements through the bushes in the garden.

Putting down the paper, Jacob smiled at her and picked her up to go and take a closer look. At this moment, he realized how fleeting such moments were. Soon his granddaughter would be older and busy with other things. He made a quiet promise to her to always be fully present and attentive to her and to cherish the momentary sparks of joy that bring happiness in life.

Worldly Connections

Fitness had always been a huge part of Seline's life. Back when she was younger, she used to compete in athletics, and she thoroughly enjoyed running. To feel the rush of wind in her hair and the adrenaline when she crossed the finish line were feelings that she often missed.

As part of her daily routine, she goes on a stroll in a quiet meadow near her home. On this day, there was a strong breeze that rippled across her face as she walked and took her mind back to her racing days. She watched as the wind moved through the trees, and she watched the flowers in the field sway to the wind's beat.

For a moment, she caught a glimpse of the bigger picture of life: Everything is connected. This same wind that used to carry her through her races is the same wind that carries pollen through the air, propagating nature.

Seline smiled at this realization and thought about how harmonious interactions between us and our environment are critical to our happiness.

The Caterpillar's Tale

Henry was tending to his potted plants when he spotted a little fellow nibbling on one of his leaves. Henry leaned in closer and watched the creature's body wriggle and expand ever so slightly as it ate. He thought to himself, *how fascinating that this plain, uninteresting nourishment would give the caterpillar all it needed to go through one of the most incredible transformations that any creature goes through on this planet in one lifetime.*

Just as he had this thought, it suddenly hit him that there is another creation that goes through incredible change in one lifetime: humans!

He chuckled to himself as he likened the seemingly insipid experiences he had in his own life that ended up having an immense impact on his life and the person he became.

For example, when he went fishing and caught a bream that had a piece of plastic stuck in its throat, Henry not only rescued it but also started to research how that could happen, which led to a long and fulfilling career as a nature conservationist!

He appreciated the caterpillar for reminding him that incredible endings often have humble beginnings and are filled with determined effort and a resilient spirit.

The Talk of the Town

Emma and her husband, Jim, had purchased their home when they were in their 30s. They were now preparing to celebrate 40 years of being homeowners, which meant there was a lot that needed to be done, including sprucing up the garden. Emma had always been very particular about taking care of the rose bushes, so she would trim these herself.

She waited for a day that had the perfect weather to do some gardening and then she set out to work. These rose bushes had been there since the couple had purchased the home and were still thriving many years later! Emma had done extensive research and learned how to take good care of them. She had even won several gardening awards because of her rose bush garden which was like no other in their small town.

As she worked on the delicate flowers, Emma admired their intricate beauty and resilience to weather through literal storms and adversity. To her, these roses represented strength and showed her that sometimes all that is needed is good tender loving care for beauty to flourish in the most unlikely ways. They were symbolic of how they had also weathered many storms in this very home but continued to survive and flourish, which brought great joy to her heart.

Wisdom From the Mighty Oak

Every Saturday morning, James enjoyed taking a stroll through the park and sitting on his favorite bench which was under a mighty oak tree. Whenever he visited this place, he noticed something different about this tree and kept a little sketchbook to record the changes.

This tree had taught him so many lessons about life. He found this quite comical: He could attribute many life lessons to something that could not say a word. He felt like the mighty oak was his friend, and he had a deep appreciation for it.

Some of the wisdom he gleaned from this tree was that no matter the challenges and storms that may befall, one must remain rooted and patient knowing that they will eventually be restored to fullness once more. Just like the oak tree loses all its leaves in the winter, they come back in full splendor in the spring and provide wonderful shade in the summer.

As he paged through his sketchbook under the mighty oak, he smiled as he appreciated just how much a tree goes through while still remaining steadfast. Remembering the adversity that James, too, withstood in his life, he appreciated that he had much in common with this old bark.

Birth of the Rain Songs

Sade had the pleasure of babysitting her two granddaughters, but the weather was very unforgiving, and they could not indulge in the outdoor adventures she had planned for them. The kids were becoming quite restless indoors and she had to think on her feet to keep them entertained.

"Okay girls, let's play a little game!" Sade said.

The girls rushed over to sit with their grandmother on the wooden window seat that Sade's husband, Gary, had built for her many years ago. The window seat had become one of Sade's favorite places to relax in the entire house. She especially loved this enclave on rainy days.

"I want you to be creative here. Be silent for a moment and listen to the music of the rain. Make up your own words and sing a song. Then we will all take turns!" Sade told her grandchildren.

The girls did not look very excited about this but decided to give it a go. And they were glad they did.

Soon, the house was filled with the sound of sweet little voices making up songs about all the things they loved. This would become a tradition for the girls whenever it rained, and they would always have their grandmother to thank for it.

The Lotus Retreat

Growing up, Lily had always found solace in spiritual teachings that reminded her of the greater purpose of life beyond what she could see every day. This mindset and way of life saw her through some difficult moments.

Lily had finally made a pilgrimage journey to the East, where the teachings that she followed were first formed. Throughout her trip, she felt a deep sense of peace and gratitude for having been able to cross this off her bucket list.

On her final day, she visited a lotus pond, which was a popular place for contemplative meditation in quietude. Upon arrival, she could see and feel why.

The pond was full of flowers at different stages of blooming. There was also a fountain and an artificial waterfall which added to the serene atmosphere. She sat down near the edge of the pond and took a closer look at the flowers, noticing how murky the water in the pond was.

She found it endearing that, despite this, the flowers bloomed and thrived. *Even amid adversity*, she thought, *beauty can thrive. And so it is, with life.*

Stories From the Ancient Trees

Marge and her husband, Jimmy, always loved an excuse to be outdoors. Ever since they had both retired, they had much more time on their hands for the things they enjoyed doing.

They embarked on what can only be defined as a woody trail. It was essentially a hiking trail through a dense forest, and it was perfect for this hot summer day.

"Jimmy, have you ever wondered how wonderful the stories trees could tell us would be? If they could talk, of course." Marge inquired.

"Not particularly, no," Jimmy replied with an amused look on his face.

"Well, think about how many generations of people they have witnessed! They would truly be able to tell us if we are progressing as humanity or regressing," she chuckled.

Jimmy grinned. "Well, if you put it like that, I'm sure they would tell us that a bit of both is happening. We always tell the kids that life was great back in the day, but they will argue they could not have survived back then without technology."

They both chucked.

"Indeed. I suppose each generation has its own highlights and lowlights. Such is the path of life," Marge responded thoughtfully.

The married couple finished their hike while reminiscing about their youth and all that had changed with time.

Dear Readers

Thank you for choosing my book. I hope you have enjoyed the book so far!

I would be incredibly grateful if you could take a moment to leave an Amazon review. These stories hold a special place in my heart as they were inspired by my dear mother, who battles dementia. Witnessing the joy and engagement she experiences when listening to these tales has been a profound source of inspiration for me.

Your insights mean a lot, and I genuinely look forward to reading your thoughts. Your reviews not only introduce others to these heartwarming tales but also contribute to the beautiful conversations I share with my mom. Thank you for being part of this heartwarming journey.

Marham House Care Home
21m ·
This afternoon residents listened to short uplifting stories which are being published in a new book next month. The stories evoked many memories including childhood Christmas times, stargazing, past traditions to name a few. We feel very honoured that we were chosen to preview the book

Click <u>here</u> or Scan the QR code for Amazon **US**

Click <u>here</u> or Scan the QR code for Amazon **UK**

Chapter 2

Heartstrings

A Gentle Friendly Face

The city was bustling with life, and people were scurrying like busy bees in a hive. Everyone looked determined, not wasting any time looking around or even stopping to catch a breath.

Esther smiled to herself as she remembered when she was also part of the hustle and bustle not too long ago—back in the 70s. The only difference now was the towering buildings and new streets—so many new streets!

Esther could not figure out where she was. She tried spotting familiar landmarks, but everything looked so different. Having walked past the same roundabout at least three times, it struck her that she was indeed lost. She pushed her spectacles closer to her eyes to see if there was anyone nearby she could ask.

Not far from where she was stood a man. He stuck out to her because, in the midst of the busy people, he had his hands in his pockets and was looking up at the sky with a smile on his face.

Esther approached him and, as expected, he was more than happy to assist her. Before she knew it, she was in the warm embrace of her daughter, and Esther felt much gratitude for the friendly face in the crowd.

The Healing Magic of Forgiveness

A heavy burden lay on George's shoulders. He lost his first love to his best friend, and they had never reconciled since. However, something happened recently that made him have a change of heart.

He had the rare opportunity to meet one of his friend's sons who happened to be volunteering at the home he was staying at. He immediately recognized him from old photographs that had been in their home. They had a long conversation which helped him realize what was going on during the time for both his friend and the lady who became his wife.

At that moment, he also appreciated that his life had turned out just as it should have because he married a wonderful woman and they had lived a great life together.

George made the decision to forgive his friend and reconcile with him. They organized a meeting and spent the afternoon reminiscing about their youth and catching up on what happened over the years they were not in contact. They laughed and cried and laughed some more. It was a healing moment that both had needed.

Forgiveness, George realized, not only set his friend free, but it also gave him immense peace and joy. The heavy burden had now been lifted.

Love in the Horizon

Mable was invited to a mixer by her friend Sophie who promised it would be a good time. For the past two years, Mable had not socialized much since her husband died. She was excited to get out of the house and do something fun for a change.

Sophie picked Mable up, and as soon as they arrived at the mixer, Mable realized this is just what she needed. There was music playing from back in her younger days, and there was an assortment of games to play. There was also a table of refreshments and snacks. The atmosphere was lively and exciting.

Mable decided to grab a drink first, and just as she was pouring herself a glass, a gentleman approached her. She immediately thought he was handsome and had a kind face. They struck up a conversation and ended up chatting and laughing the entire afternoon.

On their drive back home, Sophie inquired about the gentleman. Mable let her know they had made plans to have tea together the following afternoon. The ladies giggled, and Mable felt a warmness in her heart. She thought about how it is never too late for a new love story to be written.

Friends Who Become Family

Her best friend's birthday was coming up and Harriet had decided on a meaningful gift that would bring her friend great joy and good memories from their past.

She had searched through a myriad of photo albums until Harriet found the perfect photograph that she was going to transfer to a canvas. Harriet had been an artist all her life and had always made an excuse whenever her friends asked her to paint anything for them. She chuckled to herself, remembering how much they would complain about this.

On the day of the party, she planned it to be a grand reveal. She propped up the canvas on an easel and covered it. Her friend's children had even gone a step further and prepared a ribbon border that would be cut during the reveal. Harriet was very excited to see the look on her friend's face later.

As they finished up the preparations, Harriet felt grateful for all the meaningful and life-giving connections she had enjoyed throughout her life and was glad she could do something tangible for her friend to see just how much she cared for her.

The reveal couldn't have gone any better. There were many tears of joy and memories talked of a deep friendship shared through the years.

A Compassionate Heart

Throughout his life, Keith had been driven by a sincere desire to help humankind. Becoming a doctor was an easy and obvious choice for him.

When he reached retirement, he decided to continue practicing medicine as a volunteer. *What better way to continue doing what I love while also traveling the world*, he had thought to himself as he embarked on the journey of a lifetime going to the most remote places in the world to help those in need.

Keith would encounter all sorts of things on his travels: strange foods he had never seen or tasted before, sights that were breathtakingly beautiful, and people whose kindness emanated despite either party being able to fully understand one another.

But what stood out to Keith the most amid all the wonderful experiences he had was the look of relief on a mother's face when he helped her child or the look on someone's face after they could see clearly for the first time.

He learned the healing power of simple kindness.

Finding Healing After Loss

Sasha goes around the group asking the attendees to share their stories of coping with loss. The support group she was hosting today had a mixture of people who had been mourning for more than a year to those who were only a week in.

"At first, the biggest challenge was the very vivid dreams I would have. They looked and felt so real, and then I would be a wreck the next morning after waking up," one woman spoke up.

There were a few who nodded in acknowledgment of the experience. Another person chimed in. "I would often forget that they were gone and rush over to tell them something or call out their name. The deafening silence would then bring me back to reality."

Sasha giggled, which soon turned into a serious bout of laughter. When she finally caught her breath, she also shared. "You know, I would often leave the house in a mess and scold my husband for it only to realize I was the culprit because he was gone." There were a few giggles in the crowd, and then she continued talking. "It most certainly gets better with time. That is why we are all here to support each other and share stories of our loved ones."

Cycle of Life

Emma and a few of her friends met for tea every Wednesday, and today was no different. As they enjoyed the assortment of cakes and the fragrant herbal tea, Emma remarked, "Is it just me or do you ladies also feel like we have become the fussy old ladies who would always tell us we wore too much makeup as teenagers?"

The ladies giggled, and one of her friends responded, "Well, to be fair, have you seen how many layers they are putting on these days? Honestly, I'm not sure if it should still be called makeup or shape-shifting!"

The group burst into laughter. Another woman continued. "Don't even get me started on the jeans that have half the fabric missing. Boho chic they call it? More like Hobo chic!"

At this point, Emma was crying with laughter. "Some things will never change," she smiled.

"Fascinating, isn't it," another lady chimed in.

"Indeed! The fact that there is nothing new under the sun is a comforting thought," responded Emma with a cheeky grin. "That way, we can be certain there is nothing coming that we would have missed."

Severing Attachments

Theo's granddaughter loved to paint, and she also spent a lot of time at their home. She was a truly talented artist and he wanted to show his support for her.

Their home had the perfect attic that could easily be turned into the dreamiest art studio, and Theo decided to do this as a birthday surprise for his granddaughter. This meant cleaning the space out and decluttering which, in all honesty, he had not done in many years.

He rummaged through the items and made a giant pile of things to throw and give away, realizing that the items worth keeping only filled a couple of boxes.

Later that evening, when he was having dinner with his wife, he told her that decluttering lifted a huge weight off him that he did not even realize was there. To him, it was a strange thing to see how much he had acquired over the years without ever getting much use out of.

Finally, when Theo's granddaughter's birthday came and he revealed the studio to her, he was filled with immense joy when he realized how happy it made her. He silently thanked himself for finally letting go of his attachment to useless things because, in exchange, he had gained something invaluable.

The Reward of Giving

After working her whole life in the corporate world, Fanny was excited to dig into creative projects as soon as she retired. One thing she had always wanted to learn was knitting.

She poured herself into the hobby, and in no time was pretty good at it. One afternoon, her friend approached her looking for donations for the local homeless shelter, but after downsizing her home and getting rid of most of her things, she thought that she had nothing to give.

"Hang on a minute, haven't you become a master at knitting?" her friend inquired.

"Well, I wouldn't call it that. But yes, I can knit a thing or two," Fanny responded.

"Well, there's your answer! How about we work together to knit some scarves? It will be a relatively easy and quick project."

They immediately set to work and made fifty scarves in total.

The look of pure gratitude and happiness on the recipients of the scarves gave Fanny a warm feeling. She discovered that, no matter what, we all have something we can give to make another person's life better.

The Lens of Gratitude

While sitting in her garden with her eldest daughter, Diana could not help but gush about all her flowers that were blooming and how lovely the weather was.

"What's gotten into you, Mom?" her daughter asked with a smirk on her face.

"To be honest, I was watching a TV show the other day, and I learned something that has changed my life…" Diana responded.

"I'm curious! Do go on."

"I will if you shush!" Diana teased. They both laughed and Diana continued. "As I was saying, I learned something that changed my life: gratitude journaling! So how it works is you spend a few minutes every night before bed writing down just three things you are grateful for. What I have realized is that the more you do it, the more you get to enjoy life and appreciate all the mundane moments that you would otherwise ignore!"

Her daughter pretended she was not able to talk anymore and kept nodding, pointing at her mouth with an inquisitive look on her face.

"Go on, silly! You can talk now," Diana shook her head, laughing.

Her daughter sighed loudly and they both giggled. "That's amazing, Mom. I can really see how it has changed your perception of life, and I will give it a shot!"

Dreams Come True

Garret was busy preparing his speech for the book award he would be receiving later that evening for his first-ever publication. He had no idea what to write and, instead, he took a moment to take in what was happening and appreciate how far he had come.

For many years, he had put off his dreams, always citing excuses for his lack of action. He would state that he had no time on his hands since he had a full-time job. Then, when he became a father, he became fully consumed by that role and kept pushing his aspirations aside.

Finally, the time came when he had no excuse. He had retired and all his children had left the house and got on with their own lives. At this point, he saw the cost of not having gone after his dreams in his youth, but he still decided to take the leap of faith.

He felt like he was the definition of the phrase, "It is never too late." However, he also felt called to tell others, especially those that are still young, to take the risk and to go after their dreams because only then will one find fulfillment in life.

This was the exact story he shared in his speech later that evening, for which he received a standing ovation.

A Race of Resilience

She was in the last lap of her race. Her arms were tired and sore, but she could see the finish line. Feeling like she could not go on any longer, Martha was tempted to give up. But then, she glanced behind her and saw how far she had come. Now was not the time to give up.

Garnering up all the strength that she could wield, she wheeled herself onward. She could hear her family cheering her on and encouraging her from the bleachers, which felt like the wind blowing in her sails.

To keep her motivation high, she made mental markers of milestones along the track to have a small internal celebration each time she passed one. Before she knew it, she was crossing the finish line with her arms raised high! She had won!

After becoming wheelchair-ridden, Martha decided to keep a positive outlook on life, despite facing some challenging situations. Winning this race proved her theory: Resilience was the key to accomplishing anything one sets their mind to.

As she received her gold medal, she beamed with pride and was already thinking about the next mountain she would decide to conquer.

Journey Through the Photographs

The family was gathered watching television when Robert burst into the room with laughter, holding two photo albums in his hands. "You won't believe some of these pictures! It's been years since I've laid my eyes on these. I was busy clearing out a few things in the garage when I discovered them."

Ingrid turned to look at her husband. Smiling, she said, "Let me have a look! Goodness, is this not one of our very first?"

Upon hearing this, her eldest grandson leaped from the couch and grabbed the album from his grandfather's hands. "Oh, this I've got to see! Finally, time to verify if Pa's claims have been true about his charms going beyond his personality in his youth."

Everyone laughed at this remark as they huddled around the coffee table to flip through the book. Ingrid looked at the photographs with endearment as she told the stories behind each photograph to her children and grandchildren.

The living room was filled with so much laughter and a warm atmosphere of joy that was brought on by fond memories of the past.

Ingrid decided that she would create more albums from the pictures off her digital camera that she uses now. She enjoyed the journey through time they had taken that afternoon and all the positive feelings the journey had evoked.

Life's Unbreakable Bonds

Roberto and his wife had migrated to another country and had not returned to their home of origin in many years. Now that they were both retired, they decided to return back home for a few months.

As they traveled, Roberto felt quite nervous. He didn't know what to expect or how his family would react when they reunited. Thus, he could not believe his eyes when he saw what was waiting for them when they arrived.

Their family home was much like they had left it 20 years ago, and right at the entrance was a banner with the words, "*Welcome back home, dear brother and sister-in-law.*" His eyes welled up with tears.

They got out of the car to warm kisses and hugs from their family. The warm feeling of love had not gone away, only the vibrance and sturdiness of youth had dissipated. They all stayed up until the early hours of the morning, catching up on life and telling stories from their childhood.

As he went to bed that night, Roberto finally understood what his mother meant many years before when he told him that familial bonds can truly withstand the test of time.

Back to Center

As someone who had spent much of her life in a high-stress environment as an emergency room nurse, Mandy jumped at the opportunity to travel to a meditation retreat. This was especially so when she learned that one of the benefits of establishing this practice was to achieve a sense of stillness and inner calmness. She always felt on edge and did not quite have a handle on her stress.

She had asked her daughter to accompany her on the retreat. She had followed in her mother's footsteps and was also working in a high-stress environment.

A couple of days after arriving, Mandy found it quite amusing that she and her daughter were both struggling with the exercise to simply sit still and not get distracted. A moment of stillness was very much a foreign concept.

However, the more they practiced, the easier it became. Mandy could feel her body releasing all the pent-up tension, and she was able to relax in the true essence of the word. Her headspace was much clearer, and she was enjoying a better quality of sleep.

Her daughter was also very grateful for this life-changing trip, and they made a pact to visit this retreat at least once a year to relax and recharge.

Transformation Pains

Hearing the soft thud of the door closing behind her, Helen was surprised as she suddenly began to weep silently. She had always been an independent person, but after her husband died, her family was extremely worried she'd feel lonely, so they encouraged her to join a retirement community.

She sat on her couch thinking about her situation. She made the decision to give it a fair effort and try to make the most of it. She admitted to herself that she was struggling to live alone and that this may be just what she needed.

She listened to some tunes while unpacking. As she was finishing up, there was a light knock at her door and a friendly face popped through once she allowed them in. It was one of the care workers inviting her to come out for afternoon tea and to meet some of her neighbors.

She nodded politely, finished folding a sweater, wiped her clammy hands on her skirt, and decided to step bravely out of her room to socialize.

Months later, she would think back to this day and think, *if only I had known then how much I would love this place! This is one of the best decisions I have ever made.*

Patience of the Bonsai Tree

As someone who had always enjoyed gardening and collecting plants, Cole was ecstatic about his latest birthday present: a bonsai tree. He searched through many online websites to learn how to best take care of this shrub.

Tending to it one afternoon, Cole thought of how much he enjoyed the quiet time he spent doing this hobby. He had also learned a lot about the symbolic meaning of this plant in different cultures, and he noticed how much of a deep contemplative state it would put him in when he took care of it.

Because the tree's growth was painstakingly slow, Cole appreciated how much the process taught him patience and the value of persistent effort and endurance. Much like in life, when one makes a concerted effort, one will surely see results.

Cole tried to relay this message to his wife one evening. "Darling, I must say this tiny plant has taught me so much about practicing patience. It's amazing how little things can make a great impact on you."

"Oh my!" she cried, "if only I had known that this was the solution many years ago, I would have saved myself a lot of trouble."

She shot him a cheeky smile and they both laughed.

A Balanced Life

As one of the most successful businesswomen of her time, Margot had been invited to give the keynote speech at the graduation ceremony of the university she had attended.

She had been asked to write a motivational speech that encouraged the young graduates to go out into the world and work hard to achieve their goals, no matter what it takes. However, she took a unique approach to convey this message.

"You may be expecting me to give you a play-by-play on my career progression or to share some tips and hacks to climb the corporate ladder quickly," she smiled. "But this, you can find in any of the books I've written or the countless interviews I've had. Today, I want to share something that is quite often neglected and overlooked."

Margot went on to share the importance of self-care and maintaining one's mental health. She also elaborated on the importance of relationships and family, emphasizing that the things that cannot be replaced must be treated as such. Her hope was that the students would understand that it is important to keep the main things the main things.

Her speech was well-received and appreciated, and the students left with a renewed sense of what success really is.

Pay It Forward

After watching a movie, Evaline was inspired by the butterfly effect and how one good deed can have a huge impact on the world. She immediately got busy and started plotting and planning.

"Well, well. What have we got here, Eva?" Her husband had just arrived home after a morning of fishing with his friends.

"First of all, please change your sweater! You smell like a pond!" Evaline responded.

Her husband waved her off, laughing, and insisted on hearing what had got his wife so busy.

"I just watched a movie that inspired me to start a Community Kindness Project where we are intentional about showing random acts of kindness to each other with the hope of spreading positivity," Evaline explained excitedly to her husband.

"Hmm, that sounds very interesting, dear. But how on earth will you track something like that?"

She giggled. "I have a secret method up my sleeve, of course. I will ask Rob to build us an app where people can track what they do for others anonymously, and they can also see what their act of kindness grew into."

"Ha!" her husband exclaimed, "look who is now pro-technology! Rob is going to have a good laugh about this."

Evaline giggled and decided to call her son right away.

The Golden Peak

As he settled into bed, he glanced at his wife who had her spectacles perched on her nose as she read a novel. He chuckled at the thought that certain things had not changed despite how much time had passed.

"Care to share the joke?" his wife looked over at him and lowered her glasses even more, which only made him laugh more.

"I just cannot believe that our golden anniversary party is tomorrow, and you look as charming as ever."

"If that were true," she interjected, "why would you be laughing?" She looked at him with a smirk on her face.

"My dear, you must understand that one expression of pure joy is laughter. Not because anything is funny but because of the overwhelming feeling of joy one has that just bubbles over and is released as laughter."

"There you go again, old man. When will you stop being such a sweet talker?"

"To you, my dear, until I breathe my last." He grabbed her hand and then kissed it. His wife giggled and also thought about how much has changed in the span of 50 years, but how much has stayed the same—like her husband's charm.

Chapter 3

Lessons From Experience

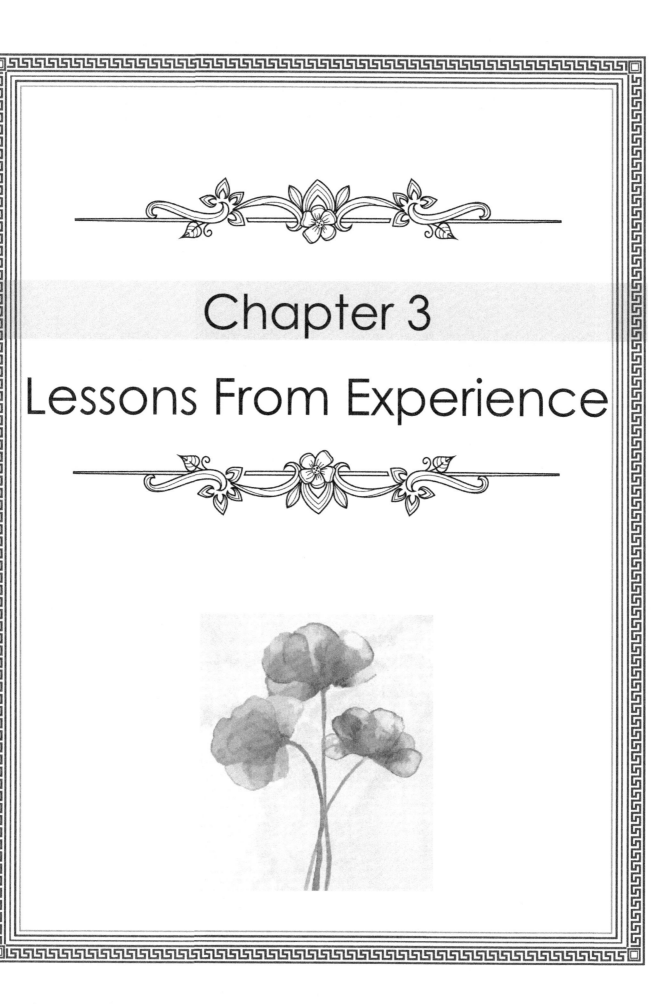

Painting Memories

Squeezing paint onto a palette, Sam took in a whiff of it and smiled. It always took her back to her childhood. Her father loved to paint, and she remembered sitting by him on weekends as he embarked on a project. It felt like a full circle moment for her, as she now spent most of her mornings, since retiring, painting different scenes.

She especially loved working on landscapes of where she grew up or of places she had traveled to. She had created enough pieces to exhibit, so she was planning to host her first one.

When she retired, she was worried that her will to live would slowly crumble due to a lack of purpose. However, she was learning to appreciate that every season in her life brought on a different reality for her. Her role was to dig within herself to always find a way to continue doing what she did her whole life as a nurse: help people. The form that this would take would vary as she went along her journey, and that was perfectly alright.

She shared this little anecdote when she hosted her exhibition, which was met with much admiration from her peers.

Triumph in the Face of Challenges

James was sitting on the deck on a lazy Saturday morning. He stretched out his leg and rubbed his knee, ignoring the dull pain he had grown accustomed to.

His son-in-law soon joined him with a cup of coffee in hand.

"You really need to get that leg checked out. I see it troubles you often."

James chuckled, inviting him to sit with him. "You mean this old thing? They've done all they could! I am lucky I still have it."

"What? What happened?" James asked.

"Well… this is a story I do not tell often, but this leg took a bullet to save a friend. We fell in with the wrong crowd and, when it happened, I tripped my friend on purpose to save his life, and my leg was the sacrifice. To tell you it was a challenge would be an understatement."

"What!" his son-in-law exclaimed, "I had no idea! I always thought it was because of a bad fall or something."

James laughed. "Oh no! It's a capsule of a time—of a friendship. But I am glad it happened because I would not otherwise have the life I have today. I learned what it meant to have a resilient spirit."

Wonders on the Other Side of Fear

Octavia had always fantasized about traveling, but she never found the time to do so when she was in what most would consider her prime.

She used to worry that, when she retired, she would have the time and money but no energy or excitement to do anything! However, at the ripe young age of 60, she embarked on the journey of a lifetime, and she did it solo!

With her bags packed and ready to go, she was met by her family in the living room who had come to see her leave.

"I'm surprised! I don't sense any hint of nervousness from you, Ma! Four countries in six weeks! Sounds hectic! You sure you don't need anyone to come with you?" Octavia's daughter looked impressed.

"Sweetheart, life is for living! If I paid attention to the nerves, I would not do anything at all. We can never run out of negative *what-ifs*, so it's important to step out of your comfort zone and go after what you want! At any age."

Her daughter's gaze softened, and she smiled. "You are right. It does take courage to do what you're doing and I'm so happy for you."

Octavia gave her a tight squeeze, and they headed straight to the airport.

Bonded Through Lines and Rhymes

"Looking back at my life, I realize that I should have always regarded my life from a perspective of decades to appreciate how much I was doing. I spent so much of my life putting myself under immense pressure, but when I look back at my life in decades, I see that I did not always give myself enough grace."

Finally, Samuel thought to himself, *it was about time we heard something from you!* He had been hosting a storytelling group for seniors, and there was a gentleman who had been attending for the past three months and had barely said anything to anyone.

"Rob!" someone exclaimed, "this is the first time we have ever heard so many words coming out of your mouth!"

There was a ripple of soft laughter in the room and Rob's expression softened.

"Well, to be honest, I felt quite insecure and shy. But after listening to all of you over the past couple months, I have a sincere appreciation that we all had different journeys, but they are all meaningful nonetheless."

"Thank you, Rob, for being brave. It's only through sharing our stories that we can build trust among ourselves. And we can continue to learn from each other and make meaningful progress on our own paths."

Healing From Strength to Strength

Lin shuffled her feet slowly into the room with her friend, Patty. Holding Patty's hand, Lin was led into a room with a few people gathered around in a circle. Her husband passed away three weeks back.

Their arrival was greeted with warm smiles and an ambiance that felt comforting. The host, Grace, was a retired therapist who held a group therapy session for those who were grieving.

Once they settled down, Grace started them off, "loss, and the grief that follows, is painful. But time sure does heal all wounds. And it's important to give yourself the time and space to grieve. It's all part of the healing process."

Lin suddenly burst out crying. The group comforted her and soon learned that she had not allowed herself to openly cry. She was trying to protect her family and be strong for them.

"Actually, Lin, grieving together will do more toward healing, so please do feel free to do that. It is not a weakness but, instead, it's a symbol of how meaningful the relationship was."

Lin acknowledged the reassurance with a nod. She felt better after crying and could feel the reality of Grace's words. She left the meeting feeling lighter, which she never expected would happen.

Moments of Mirth on a Dull Day

Harry and Maurice were eating at a restaurant when two men sitting near them started arguing, each one with their voices becoming louder by the second. It seemed that the squabble was over a lady they were apparently both courting.

"You see that, Harry," pipped Maurice with a cheeky smile across his face, "argue with a fool and that makes two."

His friend questioned him on how he could make that conclusion without considering the circumstances.

"But you see, therein lies the problem. A wise man would know not to cause a ruckus over such a matter. The solution here would be simple: Keep the friendship and lose the girl."

Maurice laced his face with a naughty grin.

"Why do I think this is not the full story?" Harry inquired.

"Well, because you know me too well and it would be foolish to end it there. After shaking on it, you go home, make a cup of coffee… and call the girl."

Harry was shocked but not surprised, and he laughed loudly, which happened to make the arguing men aware of the ruckus they were causing.

Maurice glanced at the arguing men and smiled, raising his glass to them to add a dash of more awkwardness to the situation which rendered them speechless.

Embracing the Thrill

"Come on, Ari! You can do this!"

Ari could feel her heart beating in her chest. Today was the day she would conquer her fear of heights by bungee jumping. But now, she could feel her knees going weak, beads of sweat forming on her forehead and a loud rumbling in her stomach. Just then, she was startled by a hand on her shoulder. There was an older lady standing behind her with a huge smile on her face.

"Let me tell you a little story. There was once a young lady with fears much the same as yours. She decided to overcome her fear and take a literal leap of faith. Through that experience, she learned that there was nothing she could not do."

Ari swallowed the lump in her throat, in an attempt to stifle her fear with a smile.

"That young girl is me," she continued, "and today, I am taking this jump, at 70 years old, as preparation for my biggest adventure yet: skydiving!"

Hearing this, Ari gasped. *If she can do it, so can I. I can do this!* She mustered all her courage and took the leap and, after, she also became a daredevil who felt she could conquer anything.

Cultivating a Serene State of Mind

Benson scanned the room as it was filling up quickly, feeling good about the attendance of his first-ever workshop. He had dedicated 10 years to learning mindfulness from some great teachers, with the sole purpose of bringing this Eastern tradition to Western society.

He had discovered meditation back in his 20s and he felt that it had changed his life. His headspace was clearer, he could do everything with more focused attention, and he lived life in the present. His approach to stressful situations was always logical and level-headed. He did not give in to the whims of passing thoughts or emotions, which saved him from many undesirable outcomes and enhanced the overall quality of his relationships, too.

"All mental suffering can be attributed to regretting or ruminating over the past or can be attributed to worrying about the future. But when we master the skill of living mindfully, in the present moment, we spare ourselves much agony."

These were Benson's opening lines, and he felt his heart warming up as he saw his students already scribbling away in their notebooks. At 65, he had finally discovered what he felt he was called to do, and it felt like coming home to himself.

Reflections on the Camino

It was the beautiful sunrises she witnessed, or perhaps it was the sound of different species of birds singing good morning to her every day when she woke up. It was also the beautiful hilly landscapes, chapels, and ancient buildings she saw along her way, and the mountainous landscapes that looked like paintings from a renowned gallery. Something about this trip was different from anything Sophie had ever experienced.

Sophie was an executive for a large corporation and had the privilege to travel throughout her career—sometimes for work, other times for holidays with her family. But none of the adventures ever gave her the sense of accomplishment she felt as she reached the final checkpoint of the Camino de Santiago trail.

There were times when the road would stretch for miles behind and ahead of her, with no one in sight but her shadow against the burning sun. But she had persevered and pushed through blistered feet and extreme exhaustion to get to the finish line.

It took her a good 30 days to get past all the yellow arrows that led the way to the finish line. And through many moments of self-introspection, she rediscovered her essence through resilience.

Becoming Irreplaceable in a Changing World

The new equipment for the factory had just arrived and Steven went off to sign for it. The young lad who was delivering the package greeted him with a friendly smile.

“Hi there, may I speak to the consultant who was brought in to assist with setting this machine up?” the delivery man asked.

Daniel smiled and said, “You are looking at him.”

The lad was immediately embarrassed by his assumption and apologized.

“Don’t worry about it; it’s not an unfair assumption,” Daniel started. “When we started out in factories, we did everything manually. But with time, the machines become smarter, which puts many workers out of jobs. I had to think quickly, so I decided that I would continue learning how to work with—and fix—all the newer technologies. And clearly, I never stopped.”

“Wow! That’s incredible, sir. You have left me with much to think about. I have been feeling quite overwhelmed with all the advancements in technology and, to be honest, I have been worried about my own job security. Won’t be long before self-driving vehicles can make deliveries!”

Daniel smiled. “I’m glad that I’ve given you some food for thought. My advice to you would be to never stop learning. Knowledge will always be a key to unlock many doors of opportunity.”

A Resolute Spirit

It was finally the final week of physiotherapy, and Elizabeth had just finished her session and was reclined in her wheelchair. Her physiotherapist came back with some forms for her to sign.

While Elizabeth was busy, her physiotherapist said, "you know, I must tell you. I have seen many people pass through my hands throughout my career. Most of your peers usually don't exhibit such a fighting spirit to regain as much normalcy as possible after a horrible accident. I'm so impressed by the progress you've made and can tell you have real zeal for life.

Elizabeth smiled and looked at her physiotherapist, "I made myself a promise a long time ago when I was young that I would never take anything for granted and that I'd live my life to the fullest with each day that passes." She paused for a moment before continuing, "I lost my best friend when we were only 30. She was a free spirit and enjoyed her life. She never shied away from adventure, and she never let her troubles weigh her down. Her life inspired me to live how I do now."

The physiotherapist looked at her in admiration and said, "Wow. That's incredible. You have been a dream to work with!"

The Grass Can Be Greener

As Matthew was digging holes to plant his new hydrangeas, the smell of the damp earth put a smile on his face. For as long as he could remember, spending time in the garden was his favorite way to rest and relax. Now that he had retired, Matthew spent most of his time here.

Matthew's wife came out to the garden table with a tray laden with lemonade and some biscuits. Their grandchildren were at her heels, excited to enjoy a moment in the sun with their grandparents. Matthew watched them and smiled to himself, feeling grateful for the fulfilling life he had.

"Come on, darling. Why don't you rest a moment and enjoy some lemonade with us."

"Freshly squeezed, too," his young granddaughter chimed in through missing teeth.

He got up laughing, and she ran toward him. He swooped her up into his arms and twirled her around in the air, accompanied by her gleeful laughter.

Looking around him, Matthew enjoyed how his garden had become a place to share much joy with his loved ones. Without the years of work he had done to his garden, they would not have such a beautiful place to spend with their grandchildren and make many beautiful memories.

Second Chances

The career path of a prosecutor is very much set in stone. You get ahead by making big breaks in notorious cases and making sure the bad guys go to jail. However, this is sometimes very difficult, and corners are often cut and mistakes are made that land the innocent man in prison. Unfortunately, David had made one such mistake as a young prosecutor.

Later in his career, new evidence had come to light which revealed this truth to him, and he had taken it upon himself to make things right, even if it meant ruining his reputation or becoming the laughingstock among his colleagues. He didn't care. He had resolved to do what was right.

Fast forward 20 years from that point, he was sitting at his porch with the man he had sent to jail before. They had become very good friends, and the man was more grateful that David gave him his life back and was not as focused on the fact that he had sent him to jail in the first place.

This man had taught David what it meant to forgive, what it meant to start again, and what it meant to live each day as if it were your last.

Mindful Connections

Opening her eyes, Sally looked around the room and saw that most people still had their eyes closed. She thought this whole meditation thing was silly, but she had obliged her granddaughter after she had asked her to come along and give it a shot.

She went outside for some air. A few minutes later, the instructor, Vicky, came outside to speak to her. *She looks much closer in age to me now that I see her up close*, Sally thought.

"Were you struggling back there?" she inquired with a warm smile on her face.

"I really did try, but I could not quite get myself to stop thinking. I don't know if that's even possible."

Vicky laughed and responded, "indeed, you can never stop thinking, but the idea is to observe your thoughts and not form an opinion or judgment about them. C'mon and sit with me. Let's try."

Sally allowed herself to be guided by Vicky's prompts and, in no time, she was being told to open her eyes.

Sally realized she felt so relaxed and rested. "Wow. I get it now," she said.

Vicky giggled. She had just gained a loyal attendant of her sessions and, with time, they would both also see one another as a loyal friend.

Journey Back in Time

Stephanie burst through the kitchen at full speed and had to breathe for a moment before announcing to her bewildered mother, "You won't believe what I just discovered! You remember the band I told you about a few days ago? Turns out the lead singer is Sonia's mom!" she exclaimed.

"Oh wow! I had no idea she was a singer. That's exciting." Olivia, Stephanie's mom, exclaimed. "I'm sure that gives you even more motivation to go and check them out!"

"Are you kidding? This changes everything! Now I need to go and pick out my outfit," she said, as she ran out the kitchen, up the stairs, and out of sight.

Olivia continued with her dinner preparations and made a mental note to visit Sonia's mom. She thought how interesting it would be to bond over stories of their youthful adventures and experiences. She chuckled at the thought of how young people always got a kick out of realizing their parents had vibrant and exciting lives when they were young, too. *If only Stephanie knew of my hippie days! I would not hear the last of it,* she thought, smiling to herself.

Worldly Adventures

From the warm sandy beaches of the Bahamas to the cold winters of the Arctic, Robert enjoyed every unfamiliar place he traveled to. He took time to appreciate the unique element of every place he visited and was almost always left speechless by the splendor of nature.

Traveling refined his perspective on life. He was more grateful for the things he would often take for granted, and he also appreciated the vastness of cultures. He became a brilliant storyteller, authoring adventure books for children.

Robert's grandchildren would always look forward to having him around for the holidays because of his tales that sometimes sounded too good to be true—like when he apparently fought off a lion in a Tanzanian Savannah. He inspired them to dream of traveling the world, too.

He would often completely get out of his comfort zone, and when he had conquered a previously impossible fit, he would be driven to continue seeking thrills.

Robert learned more about life despite his accumulated academic knowledge. He concluded that people are the same. We all share the same needs but satisfy them differently. We are all driven by purpose and a resolve much deeper than what we can express in words.

Garden of Memories

Rose was watching the scene unfolding from her window with one hand firmly planted in her husband's and the other covering her mouth so she did not squeal in excitement.

Her daughter's boyfriend had asked for her hand, and he was going to propose in the flower garden—in Gemma's area—which is where her mother had planted flowers in celebration of different milestones in her life. The new bud for this occasion had already been planted and bloomed, and the ring was hidden on its stem.

Her son-in-law pretended he had dropped something there, and Gemma was helping him look around, cautioning him not to break any of the delicate flowers there, until she saw something glistening.

She picked it up, and when she turned around, he was already on one knee. Gemma immediately started crying. He said his speech, telling her all the reasons that had led them up to this point before finally asking to marry her. She nodded her head crying, and the whole family came into the garden, cheering and clapping in celebration.

Looking around her garden and all the things it represented, Rose was grateful for this tradition she had started when her first child was born.

A Teacher's Legacy

"Do the best you can until you know better. Then, when you know better, do better."

These are the words Mr. Bennet kicked off his history lesson with. Although he had initially decided not to pay any attention, Christopher looked up with sudden interest in what Mr. Bennet would say next. From this very moment, he would look forward to every history lesson.

Christopher's life was impacted immensely by his teacher that he decided to be a part-time tutor when he turned 18. This paved the way for him to start a career in teaching. He was moved by a burning desire to also influence a young life positively. He found purpose in dedicating his life to sharing his own experiences with young people in order to teach and inspire them.

However, what stood out to him the most was the impact his students had made on him and the many lessons he learned from them. He grasped what learning throughout your life meant, which is why even as an elderly man, he never shied away from engaging with young people, picking their brains, and also imparting wisdom.

Out of all the decisions he made in his life, becoming a teacher was one of the best ones yet.

Rainbows and Unicorns

Rachel was sitting at the bedside of one of the most critical patients under her care, and she was reading him a story. Suddenly, he stopped her and pointed to the corner of the room.

"Look! A white horse! Oh, it's so beautiful, Rachel. Look, do you see it?"

Rachel turned around and pretended she could see it too and cried, "oh wow! What a beautiful sight! I have never seen such a beautiful horse."

From experience, Rachel knew the best thing she could do for her patients was to share in this moment and show empathy and kindness. It also gave her hope seeing how happy and at peace many of her patients would look before passing on.

The trend that Rachel had noticed was that patients who were critically ill would see visions of their loved ones who had passed on, or sometimes of mythical creatures like unicorns or religious symbols. It made her realize how our minds are so powerful that they can conjure up images of almost anything and make it so real to us at times when we need comfort.

Rachel had earned herself the endearing nickname *Bubbly*, which spoke to her kindness and the smile she always wore on her face.

Guiding Lights

Willard was taking a walk through the park when he saw a young gentleman seated at a bench, tie loosened and looking disheveled, with his briefcase lying next to him. He looked forlorn and sad. Willard decided to check in and see if he was alright.

"Excuse me, young man, is everything alright?"

The man looked up intently at Willard before breaking off into a wide smile and checking his watch. "Five hours! Five hours and 21 minutes to be precise!"

Willard looked visibly confused and was about to walk away, fearing the man's unpredictable actions, when the man immediately stood up. "Wait, wait. I'm so sorry, I don't mean to scare you. Hear me out, please, take a seat."

He motioned to the seat next to him and Willard hesitantly sat down.

"I have been doing a social experiment for my psychology class: Sit in a public place looking depressed and see how long it takes before a stranger asks if I am okay. And you, sir, are the first person to have done this since I came here five hours ago."

Willard had his mouth wide open in shock, before breaking into hearty laughter with the young man.

Chapter 4

Life-Giving Connections

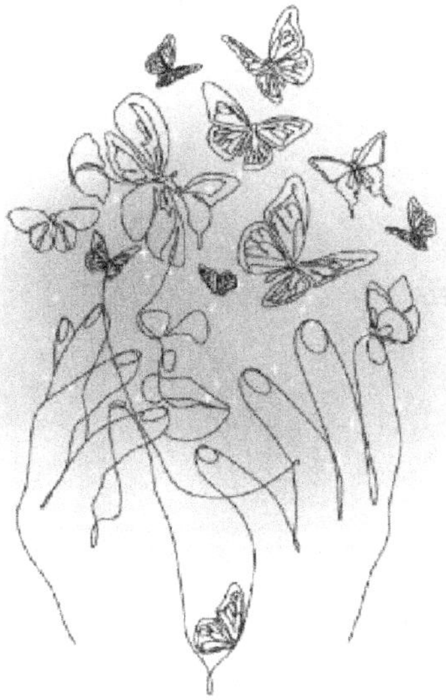

The Bibliophile's Club

Josephine ran her fingers across the top shelf of her book collection, reminiscing on the wonderful memories she had attached to each of them as well as her library itself. She pulled one book out, opened it, gave it a sniff, and smiled to herself. Nothing comforted her quite like the smell of old books.

Just then, Josephine had an idea to share her love for books in a meaningful way as she did with her literature student who would continuously write to her, thanking her for making them fall in love with reading. Surely, just because Josephine retired didn't mean she had to stop spreading the love of books.

She messaged a few friends to find out who was interested in joining a book club for seniors where they would each need to read a book a month and then meet for afternoon tea and a discussion of the book.

All four of the ladies she contacted were very keen. On the day of the first meet-up, she almost stumbled over her feet when she realized that almost 20 people had shown up for the club! She did not expect such a remarkable turnout and was very grateful to share her first love with others.

The Community Choir

Cathy's friends had refused to tell her where they snuck off to every Thursday afternoon with the hopes that the suspense would pique her interest and make her want to go. It worked.

As they got closer to the entrance, she heard a jovial tune being played on a piano and a few voices practicing a song. She thought how lovely it must have been for these young people to be part of a choir; this was something she had thoroughly enjoyed in her youth.

Imagine her surprise when she turned the corner and saw that it was not actually young people singing, but seniors having a good old time. She chortled to herself, shook her head, and walked into a warm welcome from her friends and many new faces.

The choir instructor walked up to her, "Well, hello there… oh my!"

Cathy also gasped when she saw who it was. "Benjamin! Oh my goodness! How long has it been? 35 years?" They embraced each other, and her friends rushed over. "If you had told me it was Benjamin's class, I would have joined a long time ago! We sang together in our university choir many moons ago! And now, music has reunited us."

Interwoven Threads of Compassion

Rebecca combed Lily's hair slowly, making sure that she did not pull at the tangled strands. She formed a ball of knots with the loose hair she pulled. This made her think about when her mother would do this for her every night.

Lily was not quite as lucky. Her family was homeless. Rebecca spent much of her spare time at the shelter helping women and young girls with little things that make a big—

"Aunt Becky," Rebecca's thoughts were suddenly interrupted by Lily's squeaky voice.

"Yes, my dear," Rebecca replied.

"Well, I hope you don't mind me asking, but do you think you can also help Aunt Greta with her hair?"

Rebecca looked over to Greta, the shelter caretaker, whose hair was always tangled and in a messy bun as she was always busy.

"You know what! With all the practice we have had, maybe you can offer to help?"

Lily giggled and responded that she would. When she was done, she walked over to Greta to offer her services, and then Lily beamed at Rebecca when Greta agreed.

Rebecca was moved by the little girl's compassion. Despite her not having much to give, she still found a simple way to put a smile on someone else's face.

Wisdom Through the Generations

The day had finally come! Jade looked in the mirror and adjusted her outfit. She was finally going to meet the renowned alumni from her school who had made waves in engineering and who were her own role models.

Arriving at the meet and greet, the room was already awash with conversation. She was overwhelmed and decided to sit and watch the others while waiting for the event to begin.

"Jade, is it?" Jade looked up and saw that it was Noah Johnson—the physicist behind this convention. She did not expect to have a moment to take photos with him, let alone to chat with him!

"Yes, yes sir. This is me!"

He shook her hand with almost as much excitement as she did. "So nice to meet you! I'm a huge fan of your work." Jade was surprised and Noah continued, "I was one of the adjudicators for your final thesis. Yours was one I particularly enjoyed and learned quite a lot from. You have a bright future ahead of you."

Of all the things that could have happened on this day, this is the last thing she thought would occur, and she was very pleased and thanked Noah for his encouragement.

Compassion's Guiding Hand

Dion's goal with her support group on this day was to process all the emotions attached to grief in a physical expression. She was setting up materials for a session in the garden.

As she was busy working, she could feel that someone was watching her. She realized they may have their own reasons for not approaching her and so she continued. However, after ten minutes, she stood up with her hands on her hips and looked directly at the young man.

He quickly looked away and she briskly walked over to him to ask what was going on. He hesitated and then told her that she reminded him so much of his grandmother.

When she saw a picture of her, she realized that she looked nothing like her at all, but as a retired psychologist, she realized this was his way of processing the grief.

She invited him to join them, and he reluctantly agreed. However, when the activity started and paint was being splashed all over, she saw his face soften and break into laughter.

Her heart was content. She had accomplished what she had set out to do that day: Get at least one person to make a small step toward healing.

Laughter Is the Best Medicine

Nigel had just finished painting his clown face for the day, and his wife came into the room and couldn't hold back her laughter.

"No wonder you are a favorite at the hospital," she remarked.

He responded with his best clown impression, making a funny face and a silly dance. "Careful there, we don't want a broken back now do we."

They both laughed as he headed out. Nigel was a retired soldier, and this was something he would never have envisioned doing in his life. That is until his grandchild fell ill and they all spent a lot of time at the children's hospital.

He had seen the difference it made when volunteers came in to cheer them up, but there were never quite enough people doing it. Since then, he had devoted two days each week to spend at the hospital. He was also not prepared for how much joy and contentment it would also give him.

As he got closer to the entrance of the hospital, he could see little faces pressed up against the windows, smiling and waving joyfully in anticipation. He had already started his act since the audience was ready and waiting, much to the delight of the children.

Touched by an Angel

"Jimmy, hey. I had the most wonderful dream yesterday," Brian began.

"Oh yeah, details please."

Brian told Jimmy—the care worker who looked after him—about the angel he dreamt of who came and healed the pain he felt in his back. Apparently, she had long blonde hair and a piercingly white smile.

Jimmy looked amused, which was starting to irritate Brian.

"Why do you have that awful look on your face? Is there anything wrong with my dream? You look like you want to laugh!" Brian said, annoyed.

Jimmy shook his head vigorously, "Oh no! Nothing of the sort. I'm just thinking about how I wish I also had wonderful dreams like you do." Brian glanced over at Jimmy who crossed his arms over his chest sighing irritably. "Wait here for a moment, there's someone you will be happy to see," Jimmy continued.

A few moments later, Brian's jaw dropped to his knees when he saw the beautiful blonde from his dreams walking in.

"It was not a dream, old man," Jimmy chimed, "you slept during your massage session yesterday, and it seems like you enjoyed the rest of it in your sleep, too!"

Brian burst out laughing, mildly embarrassed but also glad it was not just a dream.

Solid as Wood

Linford had always found refuge in his woodwork. Although the process was somewhat repetitive and mundane, something about it was oddly satisfying. He loved to see the amazing transformations that a perfect stain could make to a piece and how different elements could give a simple piece of wood a personality of its own.

He carried this with him into the club he had just started for seniors who also enjoyed the hobby or wanted to learn it. After explaining his love for the craft and how it had been his coping mechanism at many points throughout his life, he introduced the project they would be working on together.

Each person would get a plank of the same size and they would be free to do anything with it. From painting to staining and adding embellishments or grooves, the only rule was to leave it in one piece.

After a few weeks, he collected all the pieces and created a beautiful cabinet from them, calling it a physical depiction of what life looks like when we live in a community with each other.

People with different ideas, heritages, and backgrounds, if held together with the glue of compassion and kindness, could create something beautiful as they had done.

Before the Fall

Although she looked deeply engrossed in her novel, Victoria's mind wandered. Her expertise in psychology could not have prepared her to fill the deep void within her soul.

She peered over her book to give the room a quick scan. She observed a man with his hands neatly folded on his lap and a nostalgic look in his eyes. A few seats from him were two ladies, animatedly chatting with hushed voices, as though they had no care in the world. Victoria put her novel away and got on her feet. The room fell silent almost immediately.

"Afternoon, folks! Welcome to the first session of our support group for life transitions for seniors. I'm sure we all feel that in one way or another, we are at a major crossroads at this point in our lives. I would like each of us to say a kind comment to the room."

In a surprisingly deep and calming voice, Victoria heard a voice from her left. "My name is Dan. What I want to share is pretty simple and all of you can relate. Laugh, while you still have teeth."

The room roared with laughter, and they moved on to the next person.

Adventures in Nature

Cindy had come prepared for the nature walk. The true question was, however, what exactly was she prepared for because the boots she was wearing were certainly not hiking boots!

"And what do we have here; did you miss the memo of today's activity?" Her friend was already teasing Cindy within moments of arriving, who had on snake skin cowboy boots and an elaborate outfit to match.

"I am absolutely aware! At my age, and with my knees, it's a miracle you convinced me to get out of bed! So I decided to get my jungle fever on and get some cool photographs in the forest. My grandchildren will have a good laugh when I post them on Instagram."

The group laughed as she struck a few poses, pretending to be a fashion model at a photoshoot.

"Instagram? I thought that was for the young and energetic!"

"And who says I'm not?" Cindy remarked as she pulled out her cell phone to show off her thousands of followers.

The group marveled at her tenacity to keep up with technology when Edwin, the walk organizer, finally reeled them in to be on their way, remarking that Cindy's outfit would be complemented by nature.

Hope After a Dry Patch

It was a beautiful summer afternoon. Gloria could hear the bees buzzing, birds chirping, a soft humming of the wind in the trees, and could feel the warmth of the sun on her skin. *The perfect day,* she thought to herself as she walked toward the community garden patch.

Gloria was rudely awoken from her reverie by the sight of her plants. Several were wilting, and she could not overcome the sense of panic, dread, and sadness that engulfed her soul. How on earth would she convince the community members of the value of a garden, considering the sad state of most of the plants?

At that moment, Gloria heard distant footsteps approaching her. Without so much as glancing back, she could tell from the gait that it was Suzy.

"Why the long face?" Suzy asked in a comforting tone.

Gloria looked at Suzy with disappointment etched across her face.

"Don't worry, Glo," Suzy continued. "This can be easily taken care of. I've been doing some light reading and we could prune off the brown leaves, water the plants more intensively, and readjust their position to capture more sunlight…"

Suzy's toothy grin was oddly comforting—the community garden lived after all!

They Danced the Night Away

After nearly four decades, Muhammad was an expert teacher. His role had always been to mentally prepare for the unexpected and fill (mostly) empty vessels.

Life's routines had drastically changed since retirement.

Tonight, Muhammad found himself amid the most diverse crowd he had ever encountered in his life. The outfits, the headpieces, the cuisine… It was spectacular. He felt overwhelmed but was eased by the soft jazz in the background.

As he glanced across the room, sipping on his martini, someone captivating caught his eye. She quickly looked away, and Muhammad summoned the courage to walk up to her, despite fearing the worst.

"Hello there, I'm Muhammad. I hope I did not startle you…"

With a cheeky grin that was mirrored around her wrinkled and captivating eyes, she responded, "Startle me? What on earth do you mean, young man?"

Muhammad chuckled. "Thank you for the unintentional compliment. I am actually 70."

The lady's face turned red, blushing into her hand. He noticed she was not wearing a ring either, and he asked her to dance with him.

As they swayed to the music, he thanked himself for taking the advice he had often given to his students. He seized the moment.

Compassionate Paws

Lisa was a true animal lover. For as long as she could remember, she had always kept a pet and spent a lot of time and resources on rescuing animals. One such rescue was her therapy dog, Maxxy.

He was a labrador who had been rescued and trained to show affection and to be a source of comfort for those who needed it.

When they arrived at the nursing home, he excitedly went around the room greeting everyone. And when he reached one lady who had recently moved to the home, he lingered.

Lisa handed the lady a few toys so that she could also keep Maxxy entertained, and the two became best friends that day. When they were about to leave, the lady called Lisa over.

"You truly have something special with this fellow. He is an empath and suited for the job," she remarked, giggling.

Lisa smiled politely. "I cannot tell you when last I smiled, but today, I felt a warmth coming back into this old face."

"Well, I'm glad Maxxy was able to touch your heart."

Lisa promised to visit often, and she kept her word. Maxxy soon became the most popular visitor at the nursing home.

Dancing in the City

It had been a long time since Pierre graced a stage and he decided to do something unheard of: A musical by seniors. He made some catchy posters highlighting that it will be a journey through time and be filled with nostalgia and the swaying of hips.

He welcomed all—past professional dancers as well as those with two left feet. After all, not everyone could be the star of the show, but every role had its star on stage.

He was very militant in his approach, which reminded him of his heydays when he would be teaching classes voluntarily to help supplement the cost of his tuition for his dance program.

The musical really felt like stepping into the city on a Friday night in the 80s. It was a picture of simpler times—fast, but much slower than today. A time when everyone knew all the lyrics to the same songs because the radio wasn't inundated with thousands of new songs every month. A time when one would save all their spending money for months to purchase the latest ABBA album.

It was a resounding success and attracted crowds from far and wide of all ages who were shocked and impressed to watch the seniors dip and dive.

The Pompous Parrot

For the longest time, Theodore thought that he could only ever learn a language when he was younger, so he never put in any effort despite his interest in learning. Lucky for him, his friend, Scarlet, had finally retired as a language teacher and was hosting an exciting program.

It was a cultural exchange where those who were bilingual (or higher) could interact and teach others and, thus, provide an opportunity to use time wisely while also making friends.

The problem came when Theo came home from his lesson and insisted on speaking to everyone in Chinese. No one understood it, and this made him gloat and boast.

His wife had had enough and decided to attend private lessons with Scarlet, and then one day, Theo was on his usual rant when she suddenly corrected his grammar.

His jaw dropped and he stared at his wife, waiting for answers. She just giggled and continued making dinner while he racked his brain over how on earth she had learned so quickly!

He resolved to find the answer and Scarlet ended up giving in after much pestering. He applauded his wife for her sleek reaction to his braggadocious behavior.

Traveling Back in Time

Kenneth had the brilliant idea of asking all members of his friendship circle to bring five photographs that depicted pivotal moments in their lives. They would use them to make posters to capture the memories creatively.

There were many common themes among the photographs that people brought in, including weddings with the ladies adorned in what would be termed *vintage chic* today, children's birthday parties attended by a special guest who could juggle and rhyme, and of course, Christmas celebration in front of those silver trees that were so popular in the 70s and 80s.

Much to Kenneth's surprise, the more unique stories that were shared had common themes that made them relatable. For example, one gentleman had a photograph standing alongside tribesmen in Kenya and said that trip taught him the value of community. But the lessons he learned were similar to what another lady shared regarding her experience teaching at a school where many students had absent parents.

He learned that at the end of it, life teaches us all the same lessons in a way that is unique to us and how we reason and function. This gave Kenneth solace for all he had experienced in his own life.

Familial Connections

Candace rubbed her temples after a long day of taking care of her grandmother who was now struggling to get by on her own. She felt extremely tired but still forced herself to get into her car and drive to the community center where she had been invited to a social event.

Upon arrival, Candace could hear the music booming all the way in the parking lot and smiled at the thought of how long it had been since she had fun with friends or peers.

She walked into the center hall without knowing what to expect and was glad when she saw a few familiar faces. Everyone looked tired but relaxed and happy to be there.

A young gentleman walked up to her, "Candace, right? Nice to have you joining us!"

Candace was encouraged to let loose and enjoy those couple of hours of rest and relaxation. They all then gathered around a circle and shared their experiences, challenges, and wins from the week.

When it was Candace's turn, she shared how her grandmother had mistaken her for someone else and started telling her all the wonderful things about her kind granddaughter, Candace, who she loved deeply.

Young at Heart

"Look at this! Never have I seen a prouder peacock than this one," cried Elizabeth as she showed off her creatine.

The group marveled at her piece of art and she couldn't have looked happier herself.

"Now, imagine all the time you wasted hesitating to join this group, right Lizzie?"

Elizabeth laughed and responded, "I honestly thought it would be a depressing get-together of old folk who have too much time on their hands. Little did I know this place would make me feel young and full of energy again. Feels like going back to kindergarten."

"To be fair, we kind of are a bunch of old folks with nothing to do with their time," another person chimed in.

Elizabeth had founded this arts and crafts group at the beckoning of her daughter. She encouraged her that it was still important for her to have a social life and have fun. She shared the story with the group, closing with this line, "She said to me, 'You are still the same person, Mom. Only the outward shell has changed. Don't neglect yourself.'"

She expressed that those words had knocked her off her feet and pushed her to be more proactive about her life moving forward.

Bridging a Cultural Divide

They were preparing for a showcase of a lifetime where cultures were merging to create something unique and beautiful. Alejandro had spent his entire career trying to fuse his cultural identity into the Western genres of music which resulted in a successful and rewarding career.

He had attended a festival where different musicians from all four corners of the world had a slot to perform their music. He couldn't help but create medleys in his mind and that's when he thought to create a show out of it.

At first, it was pure chaos. Everyone had to work very hard to find their sound, but when they did, it was immaculate.

Their first show was a resounding success, and they had more shows lined up for the next few weeks. None of them had ever expected to be this booked and busy after retirement, but life isn't always full of surprises.

As if that was not enough, they were also offered a record deal by one of the renowned labels because of their stand-out sound! The band prepared a celebratory party for Alejandro to show his gratitude for having defied all odds by bringing them together and unearthing the beauty of diversity.

Perspective Is Everything

As they told their stories, Macmillan and Sandy realized they had grown up in the same town but had vastly different life experiences. This was quite an interesting fact to ponder and analyze for the senior's group, as they considered the diversity of people's lived experiences.

Macmillan felt like his small town had nothing much to offer him, and he left as soon as he could. He had seen all the sights and done everything he felt was enthralling there, and he felt he needed to seek adventure. Now in his retirement, he had returned to the quiet town for a slower pace of living.

Sandy, on the other hand, loved everything about the town and vowed to never leave. She had always enjoyed the slower pace of living and felt it was perfect for her to also raise a family, which she had done.

"Hmm. Perspective is everything, and it would serve us to be mindful of this in order to show more empathy toward one another. Take, for example, Bob, and how he can finish half a buffet on his own. We have no idea how he perceives food and how his body processes it."

The room broke into laughter. Except for Bob. He was already at the buffet.

Chapter 5

The Colorful Tapestry

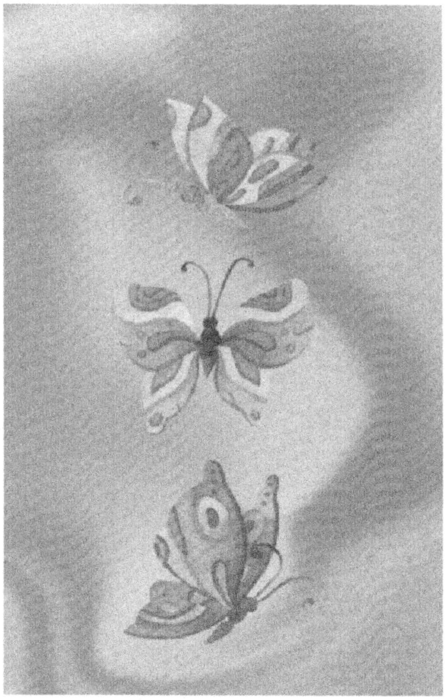

The Artist's Kaleidoscope

After what seemed like eons, Sophia stepped back to look at her masterpiece.

From a few meters back, Sophia thought her mural was 'busy.' The entire spectrum of colors. The vastness of the landscape. The diversity in human appearance, physical traits, natural surroundings…

Despite the obvious contradictions, Sophia had an epiphany: Was that not the essence of life? The nature of existence?

Fighting against her tendency to dot her i's and cross her t's before acting, she decided to open the gallery. She was not ready—far from it—and she braced herself for ridicule and sarcastic comments.

A few minutes later, troves of curious artists flooded the gallery floor. Young, old, inexperienced, refined, neatly dressed, almost-vagrant-looking… They examined her art curiously, making her nervous with each passing moment. *Did the mural convey the intended message?* she wondered.

In her hypervigilant state, Sophia could not help but notice the distinct expressions in her audience. Somehow, each voyeur seemed to find something in the mural to fixate on, to marvel at, to resonate with, to challenge… Sophia beamed.

She finally understood that a masterpiece is not objectively defined—it simply must be meaningful to each person, through their own lens.

Unexpected Encounters

Otto had never seen a glimmer so pronounced or so genuine in anyone he considered old. His grandma had virtually coerced him to attend this talk, and he was not in the least bit interested in the lived experiences of a retired dancer… until this very moment.

Resisting his instincts, Otto interrupted the speaker, "Sir, could you explain more? Are you claiming that, were it not for dancing, your very existence would be obsolete?"

Oliver, the speaker, paused, looking directly into the young man's eyes. He recalled the fleeting, rebellious nature of youth and could not help but smile.

"Young man, through dance, I created worlds. I challenged convention, I surpassed real and imagined limits, I rose to incredible heights. And all of this because I fell in love at first sight. Forty miserable years later, she is still here…" After the reverberating sound of laughter across the room, Oliver continued… "Although I eventually enjoyed dancing, I never had a natural talent for it. I continuously worked at it, but only to find my purpose. You would be immensely lucky to find half of what I did through dance."

Otto gently brushed his stubble of a beard, marveling at how life could blossom out of seemingly nothing.

The Ultimate Clash of Cultures

Isabella beamed at the room, feeling impressed by the turnout regardless of the unforgiving weather outside. This gathering was more promising than the previous one, which attested to the viability of her cultural showcase idea.

As Isabella cleared her throat to provide opening remarks, a man entered from the far side of the room holding a curiously wrapped brown package. He minced across the room and sat boldly in the middle of the floor space. Assuming a stance that would make any yoga instructor chuffed, the elderly man muttered under his breath and opened the brown package.

He got up and walked around the room, offering everyone a small piece of the contents.

"In my culture," he explained, "a man must share the kola nut with guests as a demonstration of friendship and to acknowledge the many blessings the gods have bestowed upon us."

Each participant grabbed a piece until the last gentleman declined.

"What's the problem? It is rude to refuse a kola nut. Are you insulting my culture?"

"That is not my intention. It's just that… I'm allergic to nuts."

"Well, that's nuts!" he retorted.

After a brief silence, the room erupted in raucous laughter. With that, Isabella marveled at how one exchange had reiterated the mosaic of cultures.

The Famous Explorer

Ethan cursed under his breath as he examined the damage. The sharp pain and the notable bulge around his ankle indicated that it was more likely just a sprain, so nothing to be overly worried about.

As he sat on the damp forest floor, he recalled the conversation he had had with his wife earlier.

"You're no longer as young as you used to be, love. I think adventures in the forest should be left to the likes of Andy and Joshua," Martha had remarked.

"Oh really?" Ethan shot back with a dirty look, "Thankfully I'm still in complete control of my faculties and am perfectly capable of deciding what my limits are."

Ethan then stormed out to explore the forest a few blocks from their new home.

Looking at his swollen ankle and glaring at the protruding tree root that had created his dilemma, Ethan mused that Martha might have had a point.

Alone in the forest, with no immediate sign of any other soul, Ethan got himself up and tried to walk. He quickly fashioned a crutch and gingerly started making his way back home. He smiled wryly, thinking his resolve and pitiable state warranted the nickname: Grandpa, the resolute (if not stubborn) explorer.

Chords of Resilience

Georgia's journey with singing started at a very young age, and she had not looked back ever since. She wowed crowds with how easily her voice would riff and always be on key, despite the complexities of the music.

Her whole life revolved around music, and her whole world almost collapsed when she had a terrible ailment that took away her voice for almost a year.

During that time, she had to do some serious soul-searching to really figure out who she was outside of the singing. Because of the positive outlook she had on life, she managed to harness all her strength to appreciate other aspects of herself that were otherwise ignored.

Her family and friends would joke saying that, although her singing voice had been taken away, it seemed it had been replaced by a talking voice because she did not tire when it came to telling them amusing stories. She also dedicated more time to hobbies she would otherwise never have time for.

Now, the time had finally come for her to grace a stage once more as an esteemed guest on the opening night of a much-anticipated ballet performance. As the curtain raised, she felt tears streaming down her face as she once again was able to do what she thought she never would again: sing.

A Joke in Every Line

David's son was coming later that evening to discuss his career and perhaps to glean some wisdom from his father on how to make a switch.

David was already preparing some questions for him when his wife walked in, "Don't be too hard on the boy. No need to grill him."

"Hey! Who said I'd do that? Did you not defrost the steak? If you didn't, you'd be leaving me no choice."

His wife looked annoyed and amused at the same time. "Will you stop joking around? This is serious. We really need to help him find his feet." David looked at her with a child-like grin on his face. "Don't," she said.

He laughed and told her that he can't help it if she hands him good jokes on a silver plate.

His son arrived and asked what was so funny. "Well son, I've really been thinking about your predicament and thought I'd first share my own experience. When I was your age, making mirrors was a career I could see myself in but…"

"No. Absolutely not. I'm going outside to help Mom with the grill."

At that, both his parents couldn't stop laughing and he was left confused, wondering what was so hilarious.

Friendship Circle for Life

Looking around the table, Lorraine recalled how she had met each of the ladies who were seated with her celebrating her 65th birthday. She felt grateful and blessed to have had a life filled with many meaningful connections.

She decided it would be a good way to spend time if they all went around explaining how they met. Each story was endearing and heartfelt. Until they got to Betty.

"Well, here's something we have never told a soul. I befriended Lorraine when we attended university together. But I must say, my intentions were not pure at first." The table gasped. Lorraine smiled, shaking her head and buried it in her hands. "Relax, it was not as nefarious as you may think," Betty said with an irreverent smile on her face. "I actually had a crush on Rob, and I knew she liked him, too. So I was hoping we could be friends, then I'd tell her and she would decide not to be with him. How terribly wrong I was. Feisty Lorraine held out her hand and said, 'may the best woman win.' Lorraine and Rob have been married for 35 years, so we know how that story went!"

They all roared with laughter.

The Writer's Gripe

Antoine was holding a writer's workshop that was aimed at helping upcoming writers overcome writer's block. As the author of five best-selling novels and many other remarkable works, the attendees were honored to be able to attend.

"You never have to find inspiration. It is always around us because what we write is based on lived experience. It is based on the world, nature, and its ways," Antoine started his class and then elaborated on what he meant, drawing inspiration from his own experiences and how they had given him material for his books.

One of his best-sellers was a book that followed the life of a young man who was trying to break through the music scene. With this, he looked at his own journey with writing and set out his challenges in an exciting way that gave the protagonist a happy ending. When he was out of ideas, he would visit music theaters and talk to people that were actually doing this in real life to also give his story a realistic feeling.

"Step out in confidence and experience the world. This is when inspiration finds you, and it will be a matter of being able to put words to paper quickly enough," Antoine said.

The Rhythm of Unity

Tonight, there was a full moon, which made the session appear even more magical. Myra arranged drums around a bonfire. In no time, there were more people than drums.

Thinking on her feet, she requested that those who wanted to could volunteer to be dancers and singers for today's session, and luckily, there were willing parties.

She started them off with a dull, rhythmic beating of the drum that was then followed by complimentary beats from her fellow musicians before encouraging everyone else to join in.

It was a therapeutic affair, and many of the participants closed their eyes to fully enjoy the resonance of the drums. Some people chanted and cried, and the dancers pranced around elegantly like flamingos.

When they were finished, one of the drummers approached her and said, "that was incredible! Maybe we should actually make something of this. Share it with others in some way. I feel like a weight has been lifted from my shoulders."

Myra turned and smiled at her, "Honestly, the turn out surprised me and I agree, we should continue this. We are certainly going to need a few more elements to really shake things up."

"Hmm, perhaps some shakers?"

They laughed as they walked toward the group to pitch the idea.

The True Fountain of Youth

"Amish, you are a distinguished man well into his 80s and in impeccable health. What could you impart on youth about the trick to aging well?"

Amish looked at the sea of curious faces before him and could not help his bemused reaction. Not long before, he was also in their shoes, nursing at the feet of his grandparents and ready to soak up all the wisdom they could share.

"Young lady, there is no trick to aging well, as you put it. Instead, it's more about wisdom. The distinction is that a trick often implies deceit, manipulation, defying reality, intentionally misleading perceptions… In contrast, wisdom stems from lived experiences and universally applicable truths." For dramatic effect, Amish paused and sipped on his water. "I am unwise, which is the first lesson of real wisdom. Know what you know, acknowledge what you don't. Be on a continuous journey of self-improvement, willing and keen to learn from everything and everyone… More importantly, guard your heart. Never hold offense, treat compassion and empathy as freely given and received, never harbor resentment, and take care of yourself."

The stunned and partially confused expression in the audience reassured Amish that he had hit the nail on the head.

The Memories Quilt

Olivia had never been keen on actively participating in a recreational group for the elderly. Although she was well experienced in sewing, she always viewed it as a pastime, rather than anything that could directly provide meaning or purpose to her life.

At this moment, as she stepped back to look at her designated task to create a "patchwork of memories," Olivia got a refreshing sense of perspective—the ability to look at the bigger picture and appreciate life through all its vicissitudes.

Taken individually, each piece was a stark reminder of distinct memories and experiences in her life. Her two marriages, her four children, her six grandchildren, her first career, her soulmate, her triumphs, her failures…

"I love the color and variety in your quilt, but I'm afraid I can't make much sense of it or see a distinct pattern that brings it all together. What did you wish to communicate?"

Olivia looked at her peer, and calmly responded, "Well, Cathy, that's just the point. There is no pattern to life. No distinct path to follow. Just a series of memories and experiences that, somehow, collectively make sense when put together. How it looks is secondary. What matters is how all the pieces make me who I am."

A Legacy of Love

Tony was overwhelmed by the amount of people who kept coming to his table and vigorously shaking his hand as if he were a celebrity. A gentleman engaged his father in conversation. Tony's mind wandered, and he drifted off until the gentleman chatting to his father tapped him on the shoulder.

"Young man, you see that boy standing in the corner?"

Tony followed the man's gaze and noticed a rather sullen, sickly-looking boy who looked disheveled and oddly out of place. "Sure, what about him?" Tony said.

"He was desperate for an operation that saved his life. Do you know that this room is full of people who are dedicated to donating to a fund set up by your grandmother, and through the years, it has saved hundreds of people's lives?"

"I… I didn't know that sir, that's amazing!"

Tony's father, who had been eavesdropping in on the conversation, leaned down to him. "Indeed it is, son. Now it's up to us to keep your grandmother's legacy alive by continuing to help fundraise and help people in need. It's a pity you never met her in person, but I'm sure if you look around or read the pamphlet in front of you, you can get to know a part of who she was. She was truly a remarkable person."

Finding Calmness Within

Ian had worked in a high-stress environment all his life and he struggled to quiet his mind and properly calm down. He had tried so many anecdotes for his constantly anxious state without much luck. Until a friend introduced him to tai chi.

He had visited the park where his friend said they practiced, and he couldn't believe that it was the group he would often sit at a park bench to watch. He had to admit, in those moments, he would experience glimpses of calmness.

So with that considered, he gave it a shot and he was glad he did. He not only practiced with the group but also when he was at home despite his wife's incessant teasing.

It was only later that she noticed that he was walking a little straighter and his countenance was more at peace. He successfully convinced her to join one session, but she left the session in fits of laughter, saying she would stick to yoga.

Usually, he would have been impatient with her, but he surprised himself when he noticed he wasn't irritated but actually amused with her behavior. Ian was more understanding of the fact that different strokes are for different folks.

The Art of Gratitude

As she opened her eyes in the morning, Bella was greeted by the same sight she had seen for many years, which helped her to easily cue in the habit of gratitude. She had stacks of journals next to her side table that she had filled throughout the years by writing down three things she was grateful for as soon as she woke up and just before bed.

This morning, she penned down her gratitude for being able to express her thoughts and feelings in words, the ability to write intelligibly, and the beautiful sunlight streaming through her window.

As she was finishing up, her granddaughter woke up and came rushing into the room. Her granddaughter climbed onto her lap and asked what she was doing.

Just as she had done with her daughter, Bella got busy explaining her morning routine and why she did it. The little one was fascinated and started belting out a humongous list from her head of all the things she was thankful for.

"I would be so grateful if you continued this conversation in the living room!" Bella's husband said. He was trying to get a few more minutes of sleep, and Bella and her granddaughter giggled as they tip-toed out of the room.

Making an Impression

Edson planned it like a concert because he was of the firm belief that art had to be celebrated in a similar manner sometimes. Each day of his exhibit, he would showcase a different painting style. What no one realized is the amount of dedication and time it took to prepare and perfect his show to make everything look seamless.

When all the attendants had arrived, a grand orchestra beamed from the speakers as the lights were turned low, leaving only a spotlight at the center of the crowd where there was a stool and a canvas on an easel.

Edson walked into the spotlight with his palette of paint in hand and bowed. He began painting a rendition of Van Gogh's *Starry Night*. He had also prepared an installation where the original art was cast onto the ceiling as he painted which was a winner with the crowd. When he was done, he stood up and said, "I present to you, *impressionism*."

The crown exploded in applause. This journey showed Edson that, in art, perfection doesn't exist. He was inspired to go forward through confidence to explore all his outlandish ideas. He would continue to inspire others to also be daring.

Pebbles of Kindness

On her morning walk, Lily noticed that the gentleman who lived across from them tripped over something almost every morning, which made him unhappy and ruined his mood. That afternoon, she decided to investigate and noticed that there was a boulder sticking out of the ground.

She collected her gardening tools and set to work, spending almost an hour digging it out of the ground. The young man's wife peeped through the window but said nothing to Lily.

The following day, she was on her morning walk again and, this time, the man didn't trip. He hardly noticed this, and he went on his way seemingly happier.

A few days passed until the man and his wife came looking for Lily with a basket of baked goods and some flowers. She learned that the man's mood had changed drastically over the past few days and his wife had tried to think backward to understand what had changed.

Realizing it was linked to the day Lily came, the boulder, and the ripple effect of her actions, they had come over to show their gratitude.

Lily smiled, "never underestimate the power of a simple act of kindness."

An Encounter to Remember

Emelia's corpse lily flower was finally going to bloom, and she had made a whole event of it. Her family, however, was not looking forward to it.

Her daughter barged into the room with reasons why she should be allowed to go on a trip with friends during the festivities.

"First of all, I don't have a hazmat suit and it's too late to get one. Second, the smell; third, the noise; and lastly, have you seen that thing? I will have nightmares for weeks!"

"Hazmat suit?" Emelia's son sniggered, "What is this, a disease?"

"Well, it's not called corpse lily for nothing."

Emelia laughed at her daughter's attempt at a sleek resolve to go to her friend's for the weekend. "Honey, this is a once-in-a-lifetime opportunity! I'm so glad I had you both later in life. We get to experience these magical moments together."

Emelia glanced at her husband, who looked like he was going to burst any minute, and ignored the exchange so as to avoid taking sides.

They ended up reaching a compromise where her daughter stayed for the initial blooming. Surprisingly, she was glad she did because it was indeed a breathtaking encounter.

She was also glad to leave because of that horrible smell.

Dance to the Beat

Realizing that his class had been struggling with the concept of focusing on their breath and nothing else, Nathaniel resolved that there had to be a better way to get his message across.

He got up and called everyone's attention to himself. No one looked annoyed but rather relieved for the momentary distraction.

"Get up, everyone. Let's try something different." Everyone got up, which took a good five minutes considering the varying ages of his attendants. "I want you to dance to the beat of your breath. I'll demonstrate."

He immediately got into a ballerina posture, with his feet together, and he bent his knees to signify his deep breathing and then stood upright again with his arms ballooning around him for the exhale.

For a moment, everyone tried to stifle their laughter, but the moment one person let it out, the whole room exploded in laughter.

Nathaniel couldn't help but be humored as he watched his class. He encouraged them to do their own version of a mindfulness dance.

Soon, the room was filled with people in all sorts of shapes and angles, and he took a photograph to encapsulate this moment in time.

Unending Love

It was finally spring. Maya rushed into the garden excitedly to investigate the source of the tinted hues that were seeping through her windows with the morning light.

She couldn't believe her eyes when she saw the burst of color that greeted her outside. She could hardly believe that just a few weeks ago, this area of the garden had been covered by a thick layer of snow with no sign of greenery anywhere.

"Even though this is a sight you see every single year, your surprise never ceases to amaze me," Maya's husband chortled.

She looked back, almost startled out of her daze, and smiled at him. "That's because the magic is renewed every year!" she responded.

"Well, it's also one of my favorite sights to see, no matter how many years it has been."

"Remind me again, how many years has it been?"

He smiled. "40, my darling, and tomorrow is our anniversary. I can see what you tried to do there."

She laughed heartily.

He had forgotten their fifth anniversary as he was particularly busy at the time, and that's when he had planted much of this garden for her—to remind her of his ever-blossoming love for her.

The Rookie's Gallery

As he applied the last lick of paint to the once-abandoned warehouse, Anthony admired his work. He had finally accomplished one of his lifelong dreams: to open an art gallery where he could show pieces from upcoming artists who did not yet have access to the main stage.

For much of his life, he had tried to break through the art scene with much difficulty, until a renowned gallery curator stumbled upon his paintings. His life had never been the same since.

He felt he owed it to others to create opportunities he never had, and he did just that. He was busy chuckling to himself, as an outward expression of how proud he felt in this moment when his family walked.

"I told you, Mom, he's gone senile. First, he purchases an abandoned warehouse, now he is laughing like a madman. Alone," Anthony's son said with a cheeky grin peeking on his face.

His mother lightly tapped him on the arm, laughing and pretending to reprimand him for teasing his dad.

"Ha! Your time will come soon too, son. We will see how well you will handle your own retirement," Anthony responded.

They all laughed as Anthony put down his roller to show them around.

Thank You

Dear Readers

As you close the final pages of this book, I want to express my heartfelt gratitude for embarking on this journey of stories with me. Inspired by my beloved mother, who courageously battles dementia, I've been touched by the way these tales have brought comfort and joy into her life. I'm committed to continuing this mission of writing short stories for seniors, as I've seen firsthand the power of storytelling in fostering connection and conversation. Your reviews on Amazon mean the world to me, and I eagerly anticipate reading your thoughts and insights. Together, we can make a difference in the lives of seniors through the magic of storytelling. Thank you for your support and for being a part of this meaningful endeavor.

Warm regards,

Lisa

Click here or Scan the QR code for Amazon **US**

Click here or Scan the QR code for Amazon **UK**

Printed in Great Britain
by Amazon

57668085R00071